Holidays Around the World

Celebrate Passover

Deborah Heiligman
Consultant, Rabbi Shira Stern

NATIONAL GEOGRAPHIC
WASHINGTON, D.C.

matzah

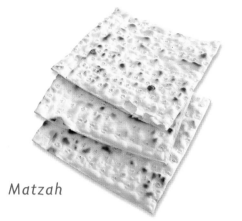

Matzah

maror

In spring, Jewish people all over the world celebrate Passover. We celebrate with matzah, maror, and memories.

At a special meal called the seder, we remember the story of Passover. Long ago, our ancestors, the Israelites, were slaves in Egypt. Pharaoh, the ruler of Egypt, treated them cruelly. He forced them to work very hard in the hot, hot sun. He even ordered them to drown their baby boys. One Israelite boy, Moses, was saved by Pharaoh's daughter. When Moses grew up, he told Pharaoh, "Let my people go!" But Pharaoh would not listen.

memories

3

They ran out of Egypt.

Moses pleaded over and over again with Pharaoh to free the slaves and let them leave Egypt. He warned Pharaoh that God would punish him, but Pharaoh kept saying no.

According to the Bible, God sent ten plagues to Egypt. The last one was so horrible that Pharaoh finally told the Israelites, "Go, but hurry." The Israelites packed quickly. They ran out of Egypt across the desert. At last they were free. The story of how the Israelites escaped to freedom is called the Exodus.

> *The sun rises over the desert in Egypt's Valley of the Kings, where some Pharaohs are buried.*

∧ *At their school, Israeli children help make matzah for Passover.*

Feather

When the Israelites rushed out of Egypt, they had no time to let their bread dough rise before baking it. Instead, it baked right away in the hot desert sun. It became the flat crackers we call matzah. That's why during the week of Passover we cannot eat any *hametz*—foods that need to rise, such as yeast breads and other baked goods.

We search for crumbs.

So before Passover we empty our cupboards of bread, cereal, crackers, cookies, pasta, and pretzels. Before Passover starts, we search for crumbs of hametz left in one room of the house. We use a candle to find the crumbs, and a feather to brush up the crumbs into a wooden spoon.

∨ *Rabbi Simcha Levenberg and his family search for hametz in Amherst, Massachusetts. Their kitchen cabinets are covered with foil to make sure no hametz gets into the food they cook for Passover.*

By 10 o'clock on the morning of the seder, we have eaten our last hametz for the week. Some of us burn a little bit of bread to symbolically get rid of all the hametz. We think of hametz in another way, too—as our own puffed-up thoughts. We want to get rid of pride.

∧ In Efrat, Israel, a family burns hametz on the morning before the first night of Passover.

> Girls in Toronto, Canada, pack Passover food for people who cannot afford to buy all they need to have a seder.

We think of those who are hungry.

As we watch the flames, we think of those who are hungry and those who suffer. Passover is a time when we give food and money to poor people, too.

∧ Aaron Kintu Moses and his daughter Simcha conduct a hametz-burning ceremony near Mbale, Uganda.

∧ *Chicken soup with matzah balls*

∨ *A boy in Connecticut helps his aunt make matzah balls, using an old family recipe.*

We cook lots and lots of

food for the seder. We use special pots and pans saved just for Passover. We chop, we boil, we stew, we bake. We use old family recipes to make chicken soup with matzah balls, brisket, turkey with matzah stuffing, roast lamb, gefilte fish, caper-sauce fish, eggplant stew, leek soup, stewed prunes, sweet carrot tzimmes, and haroset. We bake special Passover kugels, matzah pies, macaroons, cakes, and candy.

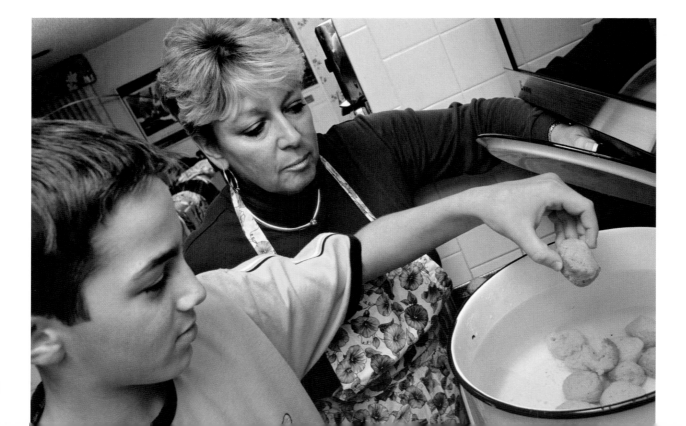

In Morocco, Yamna Elfassie cuts onions to use in her Passover meal.

We use old family recipes.

We set a beautiful table

for the seder. Some of us use dishes that are used only on Passover. We polish old silver candlesticks and wine goblets called *Kiddush* cups. (Kiddush is the prayer said over wine.) We think of our grandparents and great-grandparents who passed them down to us.

∧ *Seder plate made in Vienna, Austria, 100 years ago*

We set a beautiful table.

We put the special seder plate at the center of the table. On it we place the symbols of Passover, including maror, the bitter herb that reminds us of the bitterness of slavery. We also set aside three special pieces of matzah.

∧ *Engraved silver Kiddush cup*

Elisabeth Rosenfeld prepares
the seder plate for her family's
Passover meal in Columbus, Ohio.

Everyone has a part.

At last it is time for the seder to begin! Passover, like all Jewish holidays, begins at sundown. Aunts, uncles, cousins, grandparents, and friends come from all over to sit around the table together.

We use a special book called the Haggadah for the seder service. It is filled with prayers, stories, memories, and songs. Everyone has a part in the service. One of the most important parts goes to the youngest child.

< *The Gurwitz family celebrates their seder in San Antonio, Texas.*

∧ *An illustrated Haggadah*

Near the beginning of the seder, the youngest child sings "The Four Questions." The chant begins: *Manishtanah ha lilah ha zeh me kol halaylot?* Why is this night different from all other nights?

Why is this

The youngest girls at a seder celebrating women in Palm Beach, Florida, chant the four questions.

night different?

< *Children in Jerusalem, Israel, act out the story of the Exodus at a Passover seder.*

This night is different for many reasons: We have special prayers and rituals at the table before we eat. We sing songs, put on plays, and tell family stories. We eat reclining on pillows to show that we are free and don't have to eat in a rush. Grown-ups drink wine. But we are also serious. We remember when we were slaves in Egypt.

Locust

At the seder we recite the plagues the Bible says God sent to Egypt to punish Pharaoh: BLOOD, FROGS… LOCUSTS…. The last plague was the worst: the death of all firstborn males. God told the Israelites to sacrifice a lamb and smear the lamb's blood over the doorway of their homes. That way the Angel of Death would know to "pass over" their homes. This is where we think Passover got its name.

We recite the plagues.

Frog

As we recite each plague, we take a drop out of our cup of wine or juice with our pinky fingers, because we shouldn't enjoy a full cup while others suffer.

> *Chaya Mushka dips her finger into the wine as her father, Rabbi Shlomo Koves, recites the plagues. Rabbi Koves leads the Chabad Model Seder in Budapest, Hungary, to help young Jews learn how to have a seder.*

18

We have to find the afikomen.

At a seder in Kaifeng, China, children enjoy a bite of matzah.

After a lot of prayers and songs, we finally get to eat all that delicious food! But before we can finish the service and go to sleep, we have to find the *afikomen*. This is a piece of the middle matzah that the seder leader hid when we weren't looking. Whoever finds the afikomen gets a present from the leader—a trade so everyone can eat a piece of it and the seder can be finished.

∨ *The seder leader gives a prize to the boy who found the afikomen at their seder in Los Angeles, California.*

Near the end of the service, we open the door for Elijah, the prophet. There is a cup of wine waiting for him. We hear in the Haggadah that one day, Elijah will really come, and he will bring peace on earth.

ᵛ *A family celebrates freedom and the end of Passover at a park in West Jerusalem, Israel.*

We have

fun together.

∧ *Girls enjoy an amusement-park ride in Coney Island, New York, during Passover.*

Some families have a seder the next night, too. Passover lasts about a week. During that week, we can't eat bread, cereal, pretzels, or any other kind of hametz. But we eat lots of matzah, and we have fun together.

We celebrate
our freedom.

A father takes a picture of his children
playing on the beach at Coney Island,
New York, during Passover.

During Passover we celebrate our freedom. It is important to remember that we were once slaves in Egypt. There is nothing better than being free!

MORE ABOUT PASSOVER

Contents

Just the Facts

WHO CELEBRATES IT: Jews

WHAT IT IS: A holiday to celebrate the Israelites' freedom from slavery in Egypt. It was the beginning of the Exodus in the desert.

WHEN IT STARTS: It begins at sundown on the evening before the 15th day of the Hebrew month of Nissan, which is usually in April.

HOW LONG: Jews in Israel and Reform Jews observe Passover for seven days. Most Conservative, Orthodox, and Reconstructionist Jews observe it for eight days.

RITUAL: The seder, a long meal with prayers, stories, and special foods, with the Haggadah as the guide. People recline on pillows because the slaves had to eat in a hurry but free people could eat in a leisurely manner.

ALSO KNOWN AS: Pesach, the Hebrew word that means "he passed over" or possibly "guarding." Some people refer to it also as the Festival of Freedom, the Festival of Unleavened Bread, or the Festival of Spring.

FOOD: Unleavened bread called matzah, and food made with it. Eating leavened foods is forbidden.

The Four Questions

This part of the seder is to hold the attention of the children and to begin the story of the Israelites in Egypt. That's why the youngest child has the important job of asking the four questions. Sometimes two or more children share. One might say them in English, the other in Hebrew. Below are the four questions in English. You will see that there are really five if you count the first one!

WHY IS THIS NIGHT DIFFERENT FROM ALL OTHER NIGHTS?

1

On all other nights we eat leavened bread or matzah; why on this night only matzah?

2

On all other nights we eat all kinds of herbs; why on this night do we eat especially bitter herbs?

3

On all other nights we do not dip herbs at all; why on this night do we dip them twice?

4

On all other nights we eat either sitting or reclining; why on this night do we eat in a reclining position?

The Symbols of the Seder Plate

The seder plate is the center of the seder table. We put on it the symbols of Passover. Different families might place additional foods on the seder plate, but these are the basic symbolic items we use:

∨ *Decorations on the empty seder plate show the symbols of Passover. These foods fill the bottom plate.*

Maror (mah-ROAR): the bitter herb (usually horseradish) that reminds us of the hard times the Israelites had when they were slaves in Egypt.

Hazeret (hah-ZAIR-et): a second bitter herb; often one such as romaine lettuce, which tastes sweet at first and then bitter, because at first the Israelites had a good life in Egypt.

Haroset (ha-ROW-set): a mixture of fruit, nuts, and wine that looks like the bricks and mortar the slaves used—but tastes delicious. Also spelled *haroseth*.

Z'roah (Ze-ROW-ah): a roasted shank bone, because in the old days the Israelites sacrificed a lamb at Passover. The night before they left Egypt, the Israelites sacrificed a lamb and put the lamb's blood above their doors. Then the Angel of Death knew to pass over their homes and not kill their firstborn sons (the last plague).

Karpas (car-PAHS): a green vegetable, usually a sprig of parsley, which stands for spring and new life. We dip the karpas in salt water to mix new life with tears. The salted water also reminds us of the Red Sea, which God parted to let the Israelites escape.

Beitzah: (bay-TZAH): a roasted egg, another symbol of the ancient sacrifice, and also a symbol of life.

Passover Toffee

There are many great Passover recipes. My sons love this one. It is so delicious! It's easy to make, but you will need an adult to help you.

INGREDIENTS:
matzah (about 4 sheets)
1 cup (2 sticks) unsalted butter
1 cup firmly packed brown sugar
1 cup chocolate chips
1/2 cup chopped nuts (optional)

YOU WILL ALSO NEED:
A cookie sheet
Aluminum foil

1. Cover the cookie sheet with aluminum foil, shiny side up.

2. Cover the foil with a layer of matzah. You can break the matzah up to fit, but try to keep the pieces large.

3. Preheat the oven to 325°F.

4. Heat the butter and the brown sugar together in a saucepan over medium heat. Stir constantly with a wooden spoon, mixing the sugar with the butter as it melts. Once the mixture is smooth and thick, spoon it over the matzah, spreading it to the edges.

5. Put the cookie sheet in the oven and bake the matzah for about 8 to 10 minutes, or until it starts to bubble. Watch it so it doesn't burn.

6. Remove the matzah from the oven, sprinkle it with chocolate chips, then put the matzah back in the oven. Take it out once the chocolate chips just start to melt.

7. Spread the chocolate evenly with a spatula.

8. Sprinkle half the toffee with nuts, if you'd like.

9. Leave the toffee on the cookie sheet and cool it on a rack. Then put it in the freezer for at least one hour. Once the toffee is frozen, break it into pieces and enjoy. Yum!

The Ten Plagues

Fly

Listed by their Hebrew names, these are the ten plagues that God sent to Egypt, in the order in which they occurred.

Dam (blood): The water in all the rivers, lakes, etc. in Egypt turned to blood.

Tsfardeia (frogs): Millions of frogs fell all over the land.

Kinim (lice): All the Egyptians and their animals got lice.

Arov (flies or wild animals): Whichever they were, there were too many of them!

Dever (cattle disease): All livestock got sick.

Shkhin (boils): All the Egyptians (and their livestock) got nasty sores that wouldn't heal.

Barad (hail mixed with fire): A storm like that you wouldn't want to live through.

Arbeh (locusts): There were locusts everywhere. They killed all the plants and trees.

Hosheh (darkness): For three days there was utter darkness.

Makat Bechorot (death of the firstborn): The Angel of Death killed all the firstborn sons in Egypt; every Egyptian home suffered a loss.

Find Out More

BOOKS

The books with a star (*) are especially good for children.

*Golden, Barbara Diamond. *The Passover Journey*. Viking, 1994. Good information about the history of Passover and the seder.

*Herman, Debbie, and Ann D. Koffsky. *More Than Matzah*. Barron's, 2006. Crafts, recipes, and activities for the seder.

*Kimmel, Eric A. *Wonders and Miracles*. Scholastic Press, 2004. A wonderful book to read as a family before and during Passover.

*Musleah, Rahel. *Why on This Night?* Simon & Schuster, 2000. A lovely Haggadah for parents and children to share.

Pleck, Elizabeth H. *Celebrating the Family: Ethnicity, Consumer Culture, and Family Rituals*. Harvard University Press, 2000. Chapter 5 looks at the history and sociology of Passover.

*Zalben, Jane Breskin. *Pearl's Passover*. Simon & Schuster, 2002. Fiction and fun activities.

WEB SITES

http://myjewishlearning.com/holidays/Passover.htm
Seder customs around the world.

http://www.miriamscup.com/
This site tells about Miriam's Cup, a new ritual to honor Miriam, the sister of Moses.

http://www.ritualwell.org/holidays/passover/partsoftheseder/ and http://www.neveh.org/pesach/seder.html
Both sites show the parts of the seder. The first one suggests songs to sing with each part.

Glossary

Afikomen (ah-fee-KOH-men): A piece of the middle matzah hidden by the leader of the seder, found by the children, and then eaten by all for dessert.

Elijah (Ee-LIE-jah): A prophet from the Bible. Some Jews believe he will return to foretell the coming of the Messiah, or savior.

Haggadah (Hah-god-DAH): The book used to conduct the seder service. Haggadah means telling.

Hametz (Ha-METZ): Foods that need to rise.

Maror (mah-ROAR): A bitter herb.

Matzah (mah-TZAH): Bread that has not risen.

Plague: A widespread calamity.

Prophet: A person who people believe speaks for God.

Seder (SEH-der): The ritual service held at Passover.

Tzimmes (TZIH-miss): A sweet stew usually made with carrots and prunes.

Where This Book's Photos Were Taken

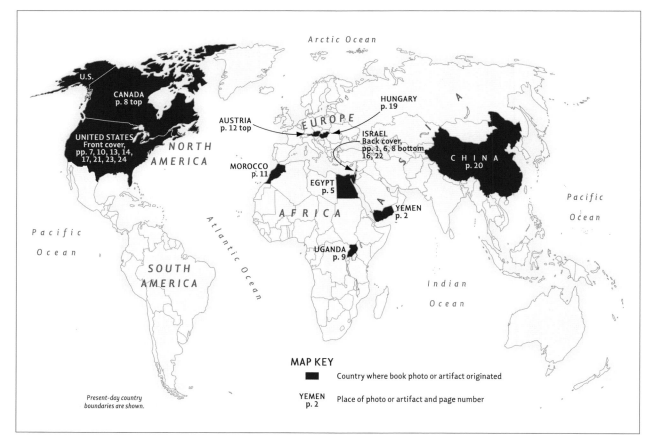

MAP KEY

■ Country where book photo or artifact originated

YEMEN p. 2   Place of photo or artifact and page number

Present-day country boundaries are shown.

Passover: A Celebration of Freedom

by Rabbi Shira Stern

Why is this holiday different from all other holidays? On every Jewish holiday we remember the story associated with the holiday. On Passover, however, we use our five senses to recreate the experience of the Israelites' passage from slavery to freedom, so that the words "when we were freed from Egypt" become real to us.

We do this at the ritual service of prayers, stories, and special foods known as the seder, which means "order," as in order of events. The seder usually has 15 parts as set forth in the *Hagaddah*. Hagaddah means "telling," and the seder is the telling of the Exodus story (Exodus 1:8–15:21). It is important for each generation to pass down the story to the next. Many families pass down special traditions as well, both serious and funny. Sections such as the four questions and the hiding of the *afikomen* are designed to keep the children entertained. The afikomen is the middle of three pieces of matzah. Why do we have three pieces of matzah? At each Jewish holiday we are supposed to have two whole loaves of bread. On Passover we add a third, broken one—the bread of affliction.

Although there are different ways to have a seder, almost everyone includes the same main elements. You will notice a preponderance of fours—four questions, four sons, four cups of wine. That is because in Exodus, God promises four times to redeem the Israelites.

The four questions: The youngest child able asks these questions, in a Hebrew chant if possible. These questions help shape the framework of the seder. The idea is that the seder will answer them.

The four sons: Four sons ask about the seder—the wise son, the angry son, the simple-minded son, and the son who cannot ask. This is to ensure that everyone, even those who don't know enough to ask, get to hear the historical tale.

Four cups of wine: During the seder adults are supposed to drink four full cups of wine. Many Jews add a fifth cup of wine at the seder to remember the oppression that still exists in the world, and we pray that the oppressed will soon be free. Some Jews add a new cup, one filled with water, to honor Miriam, Moses' older sister, who helped save him when he was a baby by putting him in a basket in the river for Pharaoh's daughter to find. It is said that wherever Miriam went, a well of pure water was found.

Reciting the plagues: As we recite the plagues we take a drop of wine out of our cup with our pinkies because in a *midrash,* a rabbinic story, the angels are seen celebrating the safe passage of the Israelites but God, crying, mourns also for the Egyptians who died following Pharaoh's orders. We do not celebrate at the expense of those innocents who are suffering.

Thinking of others and social change are themes that are made current by new additions to the seder. Some families include an orange on the seder plate, which clearly does not belong there, representing all who feel left out of society.

Seders in different parts of the world share a great many things, but they also differ. For example, Jews from Eastern Europe (Ashkenazim) do not eat rice nor include lamb in the holiday meal, while Jews from Arabic and African countries (Sephardim) *include* rice and serve lamb to remember the first night of the Exodus. During Passover we are not allowed the five main grains: wheat, barley, oats, rye, and spelt, and all liquids containing grain alcohol. Bread, leavened cakes, cookies, biscuits, crackers, cereals, beer, and whiskey are not permitted for those observing the laws of Passover. Canned and boxed items need to have a "kosher for Passover" label to be considered kosher. If it gets confusing—and it is for many of us—ask a rabbi.

The message of Passover and the seder is a universal and ageless one: Freedom makes everything—not just a single night—different.

Rabbi Shira Stern is a pastoral counselor and chaplain in Marlboro, N.J., and director of the Center for Pastoral Care and Counseling.

For my family, especially all the Elijahs.

PICTURE CREDITS

Front cover: © Paul Milette/ Palm Beach Post/ ZUMA Press; Back cover: © Ronen Zvulun/ Corbis; Spine: © Ewa Walicka/Shutterstock; Pages 1, 8 top: © Yehoshua Halevi/Golden Light Images; Page 2: © H. Armstrong Roberts/Robertstock.com; Page 3: © Ewa Walicka/ Shutterstock; Pages 4-5: © Kenneth Garrett/ National Geographic/ Getty Images; Page 6 top: © Ronen Zvulun/Reuters; Page 6 bottom: © Olga Shelego/Shutterstock; Page 7: © Mario Tama/Getty Images; Page 8 bottom: © Stephen Epstein/PonkaWonka.com; Page 9: © Chaya Weinstein/Ponka Wonka.com; Page 10 top: © OdeliaCohen/ Digital Stock; Page 10 bottom: © Christopher Fitzgerald/The Image Works; Page 11: © Bryan Schwartz; Page 12 top: © The Jewish Museum/Art Resource, NY; Pages 12 bottom, 16 top: © Andy Crawford/Dorling Kindersley; Page 13: © Ira Block; Pages 14-15: © William Luther/San Antonio Express-News/ZUMA Press; Page 16 bottom: © Richard T. Nowitz/Corbis; Page 17: © Thomas Cordy/ Palm Beach Post/ZUMA Press; Page 18 top: © Alan Smillie/ Shutterstock; Page 18 bottom: © Joanne Harris & Daniel Bubnich/ Shutterstock; Page 19: © Zsolt Demecs/Chabad.org; Pages 20-21: © Dvir Bar-Gal/ZUMA Press; Page 21 right: © Michael Newman/ Photo Edit; Page 22: © Annie Griffiths Belt/Corbis; Page 23: © Mary Altaffer/Associated Press; Pages 24-25: © Les Stone/ZUMA Press; Pages 27 top, 27 bottom: © Dorling Kindersley/Getty Images; Page 28: © Marfé Ferguson Delano; Page 29: © Dhoxax/Shutterstock.

Library of Congress Cataloging-in-Publication Data
Heiligman, Deborah.
Holidays around the world : celebrate Passover with matzah, maror, and memories / Deborah Heiligman ; consultant, Shira Stern.
    p. cm. — (Holidays around the world)
ISBN-13: 978-1-4263-0018-9 (hardcover)
ISBN-13: 978-1-4263-0019-6 (library binding)
1. Passover — Juvenile literature. I. Title.
    BM695.P3H374 2006
    296.4'37 — dc22
                    2006020676

ISBN-10: 1-4263-0018-2 (trade)
ISBN-10: 1-4263-0019-0 (library)

Series design by 3+Co. and Jim Hiscott.
The body text in the book is set in Mrs. Eaves.
The display text is Lisboa.

Front cover: During his family's Passover seder, a boy in Port St. Lucie, Florida, helps his younger brother read from the Haggadah.
Back cover: Israeli children in Gaza make homemade matzah.
Title page: Liora Halevi searches for the last bits of hametz with her family in their home in Israel.

One of the world's largest nonprofit scientific and educational organizations, the National Geographic Society was founded in 1888 "for the increase and diffusion of geographic knowledge." Fulfilling this mission, the Society educates and inspires millions every day through its magazines, books, television programs, videos, maps and atlases, research grants, the National Geographic Bee, teacher workshops, and innovative classroom materials. The Society is supported through membership dues, charitable gifts, and income from the sale of its educational products. This support is vital to National Geographic's mission to increase global understanding and promote conservation of our planet through exploration, research, and education. For more information, please call 1-800-NGS-LINE (647-5463) or write to the following address:

NATIONAL GEOGRAPHIC SOCIETY
1145 17th Street N.W., Washington, D.C. 20036-4688 U.S.A.

Visit the Society's Web site at www.nationalgeographic.com

ACKNOWLEDGMENTS
Thanks to: Rabbi Shira Stern who is a great help and always right there; Rabbi Don Weber, who can drive and teach at the same time; Rabbi Sandy Roth, who lent me books and always lends me wisdom; Vivian Philips who gave me the toffee recipe years ago; and to my friends who told me what their families eat at Seder, especially Mary Wiener (caper-sauce fish?). Thanks to Marfé Delano for keeping me sane and to Lori Epstein for sending me photos that make me laugh (in addition to finding the beautiful ones in this book). A special thanks to my wonderful family: my sister Linnie, who makes seder every year; her husband, Mike, who leads it (though now that there are so many little kids, Mike, I think it has to be shorter); to Phil, who made us laugh until he got too tired; to Essie, who puts up with Phil; and to all the new Elijahs who have picked up the job: Aaron (Elijahbunny), Benjamin (sorry about the Michael Jordan game), Tinka (a dog in a kipa!), and all the future Elijahs: Elizabeth, Natalie, Caroline, Julia, Matthew, Andrew, Katie, Henry, and Owen. And Jon, thanks for putting up with it all.

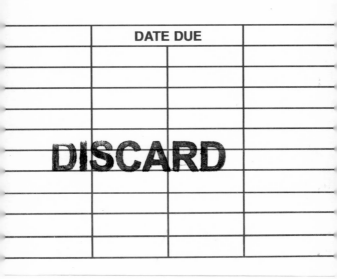

Mayflower 1620

A NEW LOOK AT
A PILGRIM VOYAGE

PLIMOTH PLANTATION

WITH PETER ARENSTAM, JOHN KEMP,
and CATHERINE O'NEILL GRACE

Photographs by SISSE BRIMBERG
and COTTON COULSON

NATIONAL GEOGRAPHIC
WASHINGTON, D.C.

Table of Contents

Foreword

NANCY BRENNAN, EXECUTIVE DIRECTOR, PLIMOTH PLANTATION

*I*N THE HARBOR OF Plymouth, Massachusetts, an old-fashioned wooden ship called *Mayflower II* floats beside a pier near Plymouth Rock. Every year, many thousands of people come aboard. They want to learn about the original *Mayflower* and the founding of Plymouth Colony back in 1620.

Plimoth Plantation, a living history museum, has exhibited *Mayflower II* since 1957. Maritime artisans and other dedicated professionals work to keep the ship in her best sailing condition. In the past ten years, they have had her out to sea under sail several times.

Staff members appreciate *Mayflower II* as a unique "time machine" that enables them to get the feel of sea travel in colonial days. To understand more about ship design, construction, and the skills needed to sail in the 17th century, they study ongoing research in marine archaeology, colonial boat-building, and woodworking.

Just as important is understanding more about the seamen who sailed *Mayflower* and the passengers who traveled on it for 66 days on their way to an unfamiliar country. This book offers new images both of the ship and of the many different people who are part of its story, including the Native people who inhabited North America long before Europeans arrived.

On the reproduction ship Mayflower II, *trained role players called interpreters portray the 17th-century people who sailed on the original* Mayflower.

ABOARD *MAYFLOWER*

*I*t was dark, rainy, and cold out on the open Atlantic, and the ship pitched and rolled. There were no other vessels on the tossing waves. The travelers on *Mayflower* were alone. It was autumn 1620. The ship's passengers—102 in all—did not think they were sailing into history. They were more concerned about the weather. But this wind-tossed ship they traveled in would become an important symbol in the history of the United States.

History is complicated. People sailed on *Mayflower* for different reasons. The passengers hoped to start new lives in America. The sailors just had a job to do. Across the Atlantic, the native Wampanoag did not expect this ship, which would ultimately lead to the loss of their land and way of life.

There are only two firsthand accounts of *Mayflower*'s voyage. William Bradford wrote a few pages on the crossing in his history, *Of Plymouth Plantation*. *Mourt's Relation,* another contemporary account of Plymouth Colony's beginnings, gives even less information about the journey.

For this book we sailed the reproduction ship *Mayflower II* to bring to life the experience of the people who crossed the Atlantic in 1620. The ship itself is about 100 feet long and has three masts, six sails, and miles of rope rigging. Aboard her, we can begin to understand what it must have been like to spend two months at sea on a small merchant vessel. Aboard her, we can better understand our history. Sailing her is a rare opportunity. Come along.

A crew of 26 helped sail Mayflower II *on Cape Cod Bay for this book.*
As on the original Mayflower, *sailors kept lookout from atop the sail at the front of the ship, known as the spritsail.*

SEEKING "NEW WORLDS"

"Such as in ships and brittle barkes unto the seas descend."

PSALM 107, V. 23, STERNHOLD & HOPKINS PSALTER, 1618 EDITION

When *Mayflower* sailed in 1620, Europe was in turmoil. Religious differences fueled hostilities between Protestant nations, such as England and Holland, and Catholic nations, such as France and Spain. These four countries were competing with each other to establish colonies across the Atlantic. The timber, fish, furs, and other abundant natural resources found there could be harvested by colonists and sent back to Europe to increase the mother country's wealth and power. The Europeans gave little thought to the rights of the Native people already living in the Americas.

Mayflower's passengers and crew were not the first Europeans to travel to the northeast coast of North America. Fishing vessels had been sailing to the area since the early 1500s to take advantage of its rich fishing grounds. And before 1620, at least six explorers had visited the region that the Wampanoag—

Mayflower's rigging was made of miles of hemp cordage, or ropes. Each line had a purpose. Standing rigging secured the masts and yards in place. Running rigging moved through wooden blocks to control the sails.

More than 100 passengers with their belongings, including some small farm animals and a small workboat, competed for space with Mayflower's sailors, officers, and the ship's supplies. During the stormy crossing, the passengers spent most of their time belowdecks (1). When not working the ship, the sailors could find a hot meal in the cook room located in the forecastle (2). Spare equipment and supplies were stored in the hold (3). From the poop deck, above the roundhouse, Master Christopher Jones could see out to the horizon and view all the workings of the ship (4). Officers working on the half deck (5) relayed commands to the helmsman in the steerage cabin (6). Sailors hoisted heavy sails with the aid of a rotating cylinder known as the capstan (7) and raised the anchor with the hauling device called a windlass (8).

the Native people living there—called Patuxet. One of these was Captain John Smith, an Englishman who helped settle Jamestown, Virginia. Smith's 1614 map of the area was the first to use the names *Plymouth* and *New England.*

The English looked to the New World for a natural resource that was running out on their own island. They needed lumber, and lots of it! To fight wars and establish colonies, the English had been busy building warships and merchant vessels—all from lumber. Over the years, the shipbuilding boom had used up much of England's forests. Forges burned yet more wood to make ironwork for ships and guns. In the year 1610, more than 140 forges in one part of England consumed 80,000 trees. To the English, America's woodlands offered a seemingly endless supply of timber. *Mayflower's* passengers hoped such valuable resources would make their colony profitable.

To get to North America, passengers and crew needed vessels large and sturdy enough to carry all the supplies necessary for the long voyage. Decks had to be strong enough to support large guns, which were needed for protection against pirates and other enemies. The ships also had to stand up to the strain of sailing for months on the open sea. *Mayflower* was one of these seaworthy vessels.

Mayflower *carried many kinds of equipment. The colonists brought tools they would need in the New World, such as nets and traps for fishing. The sailors needed navigational equipment, such as the spool of line with an attached lead weight. This device was used to measure the depth of the ocean.*

DEPARTURE

"They put to sea...with a prosperous wind."

WILLIAM BRADFORD, *OF PLYMOUTH PLANTATION*

E arly in the summer of 1620, a young boy named Francis Billington stood with the crowd on one of the many docks lining London's River Thames. A fleet of vessels, large and small, came and went along the busy river. Some were headed for English ports, others for European destinations, their holds filled with trade goods. Still others were military ships full of sailors, soldiers, and guns. Of all these ships, very few had ever sailed across the Atlantic. But Francis and his family were going to America. They would be among the passengers boarding the merchant ship *Mayflower*.

Once on the ship, the Billingtons must have gone belowdecks to survey the small space allotted to them. Along with 70 or 80 other passengers, they had to work out their own accommodations in the orlop, a large open underdeck meant for carrying freight. Some built small cabins, no bigger than a large

---

A ship of 180 tons fills up quickly! The colonists needed tools, armaments, and even some livestock, along with enough food and drink to last them until their first harvest. The crew needed enough provisions for the journey back home as well.

Eager to depart, passengers had to endure a month of delays before finally leaving from Plymouth, England.

bed, while others simply placed straw-filled mattresses on the deck.

Before setting out to sea, *Mayflower's* master, Christopher Jones, had his crew work the vessel along the south coast of England to Southampton. There they took on more supplies and passengers and met up with a smaller ship, *Speedwell,* which was coming from Holland to join them in sailing to America.

In early August 1620, *Mayflower* and *Speedwell* put to sea. The officers shouted out orders from the half deck. The mariners swarmed in the rigging. The mates ordered young sailors, not much older than Francis, up the masts to set the topsails. Older mariners prepared to haul up the anchor. When all was ready, Master Jones called out to set sail. As *Mayflower* surged through the water, the sound of the bow wave curling away from the hull echoed between the decks.

The passengers had little time to adjust to the motion of the sea before Master Reynolds of *Speedwell* signaled trouble. His ship was taking on water. It had to return to harbor twice, first at Dartmouth, then at Plymouth. The colonists finally decided not to risk an ocean crossing in such an untrustworthy vessel. They would make do with just *Mayflower.*

While provisions were transferred from *Speedwell,* difficult choices had to be made: How many passengers could

squeeze onto *Mayflower*, and who would they be? Some whole families decided to return home. In other cases, a father came alone, or perhaps with a son, leaving the rest of the family behind. The Billingtons stayed aboard as a family. William Bradford, a *Mayflower* passenger who would become governor of the new colony across the ocean, wrote that some of "the least useful and most unfit" people were persuaded to give up their places to stronger passengers. With 102 passengers and a full crew of sailors crowded aboard, *Mayflower* was ready to depart at last.

Sailors looked forward to a six-month voyage to the New World and back. Mate Clark and Mate Coppin had both been to America on previous passages.

Provisions

It took a lot of food and drink to supply a ship like *Mayflower* for an Atlantic crossing. This list, with original spellings and measures, comes from *The Records of the Governor and Company of the Massachusetts Bay in New England*. It details the provisions necessary for 100 passengers and 35 returning mariners going to New England in 1629 aboard a ship called *Talbut*. *Mayflower* probably had similar goods loaded in its hold.

45 tun beere [tun is a barrel size]
Mallega and Canari caske 16 a tun [kinds of wine]
6 tuns of water
12 M of bread, after ³/₄ C. to a man [M=1,000 pounds; C=100 pounds]
22 hheds of bieffe [hheds stands for hogshead, a barrel size]
40 bushells peas, a peck a man ye voyadg
20 bushells oatmeale
14 C. haberdyne [kind of fish]
8 dussen pounds of candeles
2 terces of beere vyneger [terce is a barrel size]
1 ¹/₂ bushels mustard seede
20 gallons oyle, Gallipoly or Mayorke, a qrt a man
2 ferkins [firkins, a barrel size] of soape
2 runlett Spanish wyne, 10 galls a p [runlett is a barrel size]
4 thowsand of billets [firewood]
10 firkins of butter
10 C. of cheese
20 gallons aquavite [a type of liquor]

Sailors used block and tackle to load supplies into the hold of Mayflower.
Water and beer for the voyage were contained in barrels. Supplies that needed to be kept dry, such as salted fish, were also stored in barrels.

A VARIED COMPANY

"Readier to go to dispute than to set forward a voyage."

COLONIST ROBERT CUSHMAN, LETTER OF JUNE 10, 1620, WRITTEN WHILE PURCHASING PROVISIONS

*P*opular myth describes the passengers aboard *Mayflower* as a band of brave Pilgrims setting sail to gain religious freedom in the New World. In reality, they were not a unified group, and they never called themselves Pilgrims. That name was applied two centuries later by historians who took it from William Bradford's *Of Plymouth Plantation*. In a brief passage, Bradford had identified members of his church as pilgrims in a religious sense—that is, they were on a journey seeking God. He never meant his biblical reference to include everyone on board.

Bradford was a leader of a congregation of British Protestants, sometimes called Puritans or Separatists, who had broken away from the national Church of England. Persecuted for their way of worship, they had fled England in 1609 for Holland. After living in exile in the city of Leiden for more than ten years, some

---

Aboard Mayflower *to do a job, not found a colony, the sailors sometimes troubled the passengers with insults and frightening tales. Children had to endure long hours in close quarters during bad weather.*

of the church members decided to sail to America to found a colony.

To finance the voyage, the Leiden church members made a deal with a group of English investors known as merchant adventurers. The merchants agreed to pay for the ship and supplies, and the colonists signed a contract promising to work in North America to pay them back. From the start the colonists argued with the investors

In fair weather, passengers were invited to exercise on deck and enjoy fresh air and sunlight. Belowdecks, familiar tasks such as knitting, as well as games and stories, helped to pass the time.

about how much to spend on provisions and about the terms of their contract.

Everyone aboard *Mayflower* hoped to own land and provide a good future for their children. More than half the families had some connection with the Leiden church, and several others may well have agreed with them about the need for religious reform. At least a few, however, were suspicious of Puritans and hostile to the colony's leaders. These differences led to tensions. William Bradford complained about "untoward [difficult and unruly] persons," and identified the Billington family as "one of the profanest [most disrespectful of religion]." He wondered how the Billingtons had been "shuffled into their company."

The colonists differed in other ways as well. They disagreed about who should be allowed to own land and how to organize the group for work once they arrived in the New World. Shopkeepers and tradesmen came from cities and towns, while farmers came from the countryside. The colonists came from many regions and spoke an assortment of dialects. Like their countrymen in England, some knew how to read, while others didn't. None were lords. Some families brought servants; most did not. The colonists did not regard themselves as a group of equals. They reflected the variety found in the middle and lower classes of 17th-century English society.

NORTH AMERICA

PATUXET/
New Plymouth

Area enlarged,
below left

PACIFIC OCEAN

ATLANTIC OCEAN

EQUATOR

SOUTH AMERICA

⑪ Patuxet/ New Plymouth

On December 11, the shallop landed at the place known to the Wampanoag as Patuxet, which the English called New Plymouth. *Mayflower* followed, arriving on December 16.

⑩ First anchorage

Mayflower anchored November 11, 1620, and the colonists soon started exploring Cape Cod in a small open boat called a shallop. On December 6, a large party of men set out in the shallop on their longest "discovery."

⑨ Landfall

Headed south for the Hudson River, *Mayflower* ran into dangerous shoals, or sandbars, and turned back.

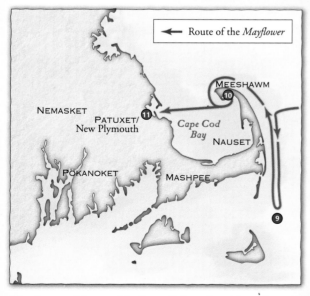

← Route of the *Mayflower*

NEMASKET
PATUXET/
New Plymouth
MEESHAWM
⑩
Cape Cod Bay
NAUSET
POKANOKET
MASHPEE
⑪
⑨

Meeshawm, Nauset, Mashpee, Pokanoket, Nemasket, and Patuxet are six of the 67 Wampanoag towns existing prior to Mayflower's arrival.

Scale at Equator

0   500   1,000 miles

0   500   1,000 kilometers

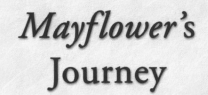

Mayflower's Journey

EUROPE

Great Britain

Plymouth

Area enlarged, below right

ASIA

AFRICA

❶ *Scrooby*

In 1607, Richard Clyfton and John Robinson led some 100 members of their outlawed religious congregation from Scrooby into exile in Amsterdam. Holland was well known as a country that tolerated different religions. Among the congregation were future colonial leaders John Carver, William Brewster, and William Bradford.

❷ *Amsterdam*

In 1609–1610, after disputes with other exiled English churches in Amsterdam, John Robinson led a congregation that settled in Leiden, another town in Holland.

❸ *Leiden*

By 1616, members of the Leiden church were unhappy with life in Holland and began to think about moving to America. After a few unsuccessful proposals, they began talks with Englishman Thomas Weston about founding a new colony.

❹ *London*

In the spring of 1620, Thomas Weston and about 70 other investors put up money to begin a colony in North America. At least 50 people from England were ready to join members of the Leiden church in the venture.

❺ *Delftshaven*

Early in the summer of 1620, members of the Leiden church purchased a small ship, *Speedwell*, "of some 60 tun," compared to *Mayflower*'s 180. They boarded in this Dutch port and sailed to Southampton in England to meet *Mayflower*. They hoped to sail the two ships together across the Atlantic.

→ Route of the *Mayflower*

Scrooby **❶**

Great Britain

Amsterdam **❷**
Leiden **❸**
Delftshaven **❺**

London **❹**

Southampton **❻**

Plymouth **❽** **❼** Dartmouth

English Channel

E U R O P E

❽ *Plymouth*

After further troubles with *Speedwell*, the colonists decided to leave that ship behind. They chose from among them 102 passengers, who crowded aboard *Mayflower* and finally departed on September 6, 1620.

❼ *Dartmouth*

With *Speedwell* leaking, the two ships put in at Dartmouth for repairs, setting out again a few weeks later.

❻ *Southampton*

In late July, *Mayflower* and *Speedwell* took on final supplies and passengers. Despite disagreements about money, supplies, and their contract, the colonists at last departed on August 5, 1620.

The Voyage

"...the vast ocean, and a sea of troubles...."

WILLIAM BRADFORD, *OF PLYMOUTH PLANTATION*

O n September 6, 1620, *Mayflower* left the dock at Plymouth, England, and set out alone for the New World. All the passengers had experienced at least two other ship departures by then and must have begun to see familiar patterns. What appeared to be chaos among men and rigging slowly evolved into the smooth operation of a ship under sail. The passengers must have felt encouraged by the week of fair weather they had at the start of their voyage. Some of them could handle the constant motion of the ship, whereas others, even in calm weather, were seasick.

Soon autumn gales began to blow. As William Bradford told it, "They were encountered many times with crosswinds and met with fierce storms, with which the ship was shroudly [viciously] shaken, and her upper works made very leaky." Several accounts tell of ships in the 17th century that suffered damage in storms.

Few of Mayflower's *passengers had been to sea before. Weeks of rough weather and wet conditions belowdecks made many people sick. Some passengers stayed weak and ill even after the ship arrived in America.*

Passenger John Howland had to be helped back aboard after being pitched into the sea by the wildly tossing Mayflower.

Some vessels lost their masts and rigging to the sea. One ill-fated ship lost its entire forward cabin, including the cook room and all the people working there. By comparison, *Mayflower* was lucky. During her stormy passage she suffered only a bowed and cracked main deck beam. While this frightened some mariners and passengers enough to suggest turning back to England, the ship's carpenter quickly had the damaged beam repaired.

Still, the danger to the passengers and crew remained. Bradford relates that "in sundry of these storms the winds were so fierce and the seas so high, as they could not bear a knot of sail, but were forced thus to hull [to ride out a storm with no sails set] for divers days together." And in one of the storms, "John Howland, coming upon some occasion above the gratings was, with a seele [tipping] of the ship, thrown into the sea." According to Bradford, "it pleased God that he caught hold of the topsail halyards [long ropes]," which had worked loose in the storm and happened to be trailing in the water. Sailors were then able to pull him back aboard.

During the rough weather, conditions aboard *Mayflower* became increasingly wet and miserable. The air belowdecks smelled foul. Amid the cramped

Sailors constantly worked to keep a ship seaworthy. The crew stayed busy repairing sails, sealing up decks with caulking, and keeping everything secure on the aging Mayflower.

One passenger, William Butten, and one sailor died during the crossing. Their bodies were wrapped in shrouds and dropped overboard. Travel at sea in the 17th century was considered so difficult and dangerous that shipboard deaths were not unexpected. Many Mayflower passengers sought comfort in worship and prayer.

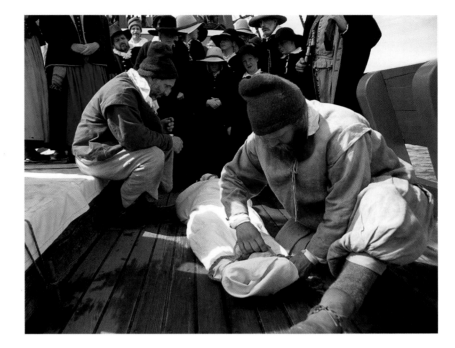

Hot meals, such as pottage (stew), could be cooked only in calm weather, so passengers often ate cold food. Everyone, including children, drank beer. Reading helped pass the time.

animal pens and crowded cabins, many passengers fell sick. Yet they felt blessed that only one colonist, William Butten, a servant in the Fuller family, died at sea. A sailor also died on the voyage. Some of the passengers observed that this sailor had been the worst in ridiculing the frightened colonists. They believed his death showed the just hand of God at work.

In fair weather, the passengers were allowed up on deck to get fresh air and exercise. Young Francis Billington was probably among them. But in the long spells of bad weather that plagued the two-month crossing, they must have spent many uncomfortable hours cooped up belowdecks. The religious tensions existing between the colonists may have occasionally troubled them. Still, they entertained themselves as well as they could by playing simple games, reading, singing, and telling stories and riddles. One happy event was the birth of Elizabeth Hopkins's son, appropriately named Oceanus.

As *Mayflower* drew closer to land in early November, Master Jones sent sailors aloft as lookouts. Finally, the mariners spotted the high dunes of

Cape Cod, in the place now known as Massachusetts. They were happy to see land, even though they were about 200 miles northeast of their intended destination. The colonists' contract had granted them land near the Hudson River, so the ship headed south. After trying to sail in dangerously shallow waters in unfavorable winds, Master Jones turned the ship around and brought her to anchor in the harbor at the tip of Cape Cod.

The Mayflower *voyage was long, and there were about 30 children aboard with very little space for play. Nine Men's Morris was a popular children's game that could be played in tight quarters.*

Navigation in the 17th Century

When beyond sight of land, *Mayflower*'s Master Jones relied on his navigational skills and only a few tools to help him reach shore again. He kept the ship on course by using a magnetic compass. To determine latitude—the position north or south of the Equator—he used a cross staff. This tool consisted of a short crosspiece that slid on a long stick marked in degrees. Near noon, the master repeatedly measured the height of the sun by holding the long stick just below his eye and sliding the crosspiece back and forth until it lined up with the sun on the top and the horizon on the bottom. He then noted the angle. After consulting a book of numerical tables and performing some calculations, he could determine the ship's latitude for the day.

He used a chip log to estimate the ship's speed. This small, flat piece of wood attached to a long line on a reel was thrown overboard and floated behind as *Mayflower* sailed ahead. By counting evenly spaced knots in the line as they passed through his hand in a known length of time, the master calculated the speed of the ship in knots, or nautical miles per hour. By multiplying the speed by the number of hours sailed, he could plot the course his ship had covered. He made a series of marks that marched across his chart of the ocean, hoping they would steer him to a safe landfall.

Navigation methods in the 17th century were far from precise. Even skilled navigators could end up off course. With help from two mates who had sailed to America previously, Master Jones landed only one degree north of his goal.

LANDFALL

"...thus arrived in a good harbor and brought safe to land..."

WILLIAM BRADFORD, *OF PLYMOUTH PLANTATION*

*J*t is hard to imagine how it felt to reach land after two months of a dangerous sea voyage. William Bradford wrote: "...[A]fter long beating at sea they fell with that land which is called Cape Cod;...[and] they were not a little joyful....they fell upon their knees, and blessed the God of Heaven, who had brought them over the vast and furious ocean, and delivered them from all the perils and miseries thereof."

Even before going ashore, Francis Billington may have overheard his father muttering to a few other colonists about their contract. Since Cape Cod was north of the specified boundaries, some colonists doubted that the original contract still applied. The leaders of the colony feared that such men might refuse to be governed. To prevent disorder, they restated the terms of the contract in a brief, written agreement that had to be signed before anyone went ashore. This emphasized

---

When lookouts finally spotted land, both passengers and crew rejoiced. A small workboat called a shallop, which had been stored on Mayflower, *was soon put to use as colonists began exploring Cape Cod for a suitable place to build their new colony.*

"submission and obedience" to God, the English king, and the company of merchant investors that had granted the colonists permission to settle in English territory. Almost 200 years later, this document became famous as the "Mayflower Compact" when 19th-century historians mistakenly thought they had discovered the beginnings of democracy in it.

Once the ship had anchored, the colonists had much to do. They were happy to be able to get outside, away from their smelly quarters belowdecks. Sailors rowed the women ashore to wash and air clothes. Some of the men set to work repairing the colonists' shallop, the workboat that had been stowed in the passenger quarters. It had been damaged by people sleeping in it during the voyage. Once seaworthy, the shallop would be needed to explore the curving coastline of Cape Cod as the colonists searched for a good place to build their houses before winter arrived.

Some of the men began going on land with armor and muskets. They discovered empty Wampanoag homes and took food, bowls, baskets, and other appealing things from them. They also dug up stores of buried corn, as well as Wampanoag graves. Few of the colonists considered this stealing. Most of them had little or no respect for those they called *Indians* or *savages*.

Before going ashore, colonists had to sign a document drawn up by colony leaders after arrival at Cape Cod. It restated the contract and upheld the leaders' authority.

Well-armed exploring parties waded ashore at Cape Cod and surveyed the coast. Some goods and animals were carried from Mayflower *onto dry land.*

Francis Billington got into mischief aboard *Mayflower* in early December. Perhaps he was bored after being confined on the ship for so long. *Mourt's Relation,* a 1622 book about Plymouth Colony, related the incident: "We, through God's mercy, escaped a great danger by the foolishness of a boy, one of…Billington's sons." Francis had shot off his father's gun, "…the fire being within four feet of the bed between the decks…and many people about the fire, and yet, by God's mercy, no harm done."

While the colonists explored Cape Cod, their disrespect for homes and burial grounds provoked some Wampanoag men to shoot arrows at them near Nauset Beach. The Wampanoag were understandably outraged: Europeans from previous ships had brought strange diseases and even kidnapped many of their people. The colonists returned fire with their muskets, but there were no casualties on either side.

After spending a few weeks in Cape Cod, the *Mayflower* passengers decided to look for another place to build their colony. The exploring party boarded the shallop and headed for a harbor across the bay. In a fierce snowstorm, the boat was nearly lost. At nightfall, however, they landed safely on a small island just offshore. The next day, Sunday, was spent in worship and rest. On the following day, the colonists sailed farther into the harbor, hoping to find a good place to settle.

When Mayflower *colonists discovered a supply of dried corn buried at Cape Cod, they dug it up and carried it away. The men brought many of the objects they found back to the ship for everyone to look at. The Native people considered this stealing.*

An Established Nation

Sometimes people say that a person "came over on the *Mayflower*" to indicate that he or she is a member of a very old American family. But the Wampanoag had lived in America long before *Mayflower*'s arrival. For some 12,000 years they had fished the waters, hunted the shores, and planted crops in the sheltered inland areas. Their name means "People of the First Light," but they referred to themselves simply as the People. Their territory was large. It stretched from what is now called Grafton, Massachusetts, to the southeastern corner of Rhode Island and across Cape Cod, Nantucket, and Martha's Vineyard. Their rich culture was organized around family, village, and nation. Their leaders, called sachems, governed by general agreement.

The *Mayflower* colonists were not the first Europeans in Wampanoag territory. Earlier explorers brought trade to the area. They also brought diseases, including plague, which swept through the land from 1616 to 1618. By the time *Mayflower* arrived, sickness had killed so many in Patuxet—the place called Plymouth by the English—that no Wampanoag were left there. To the People, the empty village was a reminder of tragedy and loss. To the colonists, finding tilled fields was a sign of God's favor. They gave little thought to those whose land they were taking over.

Native people had lived in harmony with the land in North America for at least 12,000 years before Europeans arrived.

SETTLEMENT AT "A MOST HOPEFUL PLACE"

*O*n Monday, December 11, 1620, the exploring party from *Mayflower* landed the shallop at the place they would call Plymouth. There is no record that anyone stepped from the boat onto a large rock—later called Plymouth Rock—at this time, but come ashore they did. The colonists found streams with fresh running water, cleared fields, and a good hill for mounting their cannon. To them, it seemed "a most hopeful place" to settle.

The colonists began construction of their new community in late December. A long, cold winter lay ahead. By springtime, half the colonists and half the sailors had perished from exposure, malnutrition, or illness. Despite these hardships, the survivors continued to build their settlement.

In January 1621, young Francis Billington made a discovery of his own in his new home. As told in *Mourt's Relation*, Francis climbed a tree near Plymouth and sighted a large pond, "a great sea as he thought…full of fish and fowl…an excellent help for us in time." Looking around from his treetop perch, Francis would also have seen *Mayflower*, still moored behind him in the bay. The ship would remain there until April 5, 1621, when Master Jones and his crew sailed back to England. Not one of the colonists went along. They were determined to make this land their home.

Working quickly to raise shelter before winter set in, the settlers built small wooden houses, using reeds to thatch the roofs. During that first winter, many colonists still slept aboard Mayflower *at night.*

BRINGING THE PAST TO LIFE

In April 1621, *Mayflower* sailed back to England. She never returned to North America and was eventually sold for scrap. But since 1957 another ship, *Mayflower II,* has attracted millions of visitors to Plimoth Plantation. Here they learn not only about the reproduction vessel, but also about the significance of the original ship in the context of America's colonial history.

In the summer of 2001, a well-trained crew of staff and volunteers from Plimoth Plantation sailed *Mayflower II* from Plymouth to Boston, Massachusetts. A photography team from National Geographic went along. The purpose of the sail was to create the scenes you have seen in the pages of this book—scenes re-created from the *Mayflower* sail of 1620, nearly 400 years earlier. To curious onlookers aboard the many modern boats that motored alongside the ship as she arrived in Boston, *Mayflower II* must have looked like a visitor from the distant past. And in a way, she is. *Mayflower II* and her staff tell a story about a time in

history when enormous changes came to North America.

The meaning of these changes was vastly different for the colonists and the Native people who had already lived for many thousands of years in the so-called New World. For the colonists, the 1620 *Mayflower* was a means of beginning a new life, as well as a link with their home back in Europe. For Native people, the ship was an instrument of change forcing its way into their world—and nearly destroying it. Plimoth Plantation is dedicated to helping modern people reach a better understanding of all facets of our colonial past.

Mayflower II, *shown here at her dock in Plymouth, Massachusetts, sailed from Plymouth to Boston in 2001. Garbed in reproduction colonial-era clothing, interpreters re-created scenes from the first* Mayflower's *voyage.*

as almost a year's
turned to a group of
"joint stock" com-
he money and the
bought supplies for
ools and food enough
ds were loaded into
selves as comfortable
ted cabins. Period
ot passengers.

A fireboat sprays water to welcome
Mayflower II *into Boston Harbor in
2001 (above). A dockside exhibit greets
visitors to* Mayflower II *at her berth
in Plymouth (near left). Nearby,
tourists peer down at Plymouth Rock,
where the Pilgrims are traditionally
thought to have landed in 1620 (far
left). It is uncertain whether the*
Mayflower *colonists stepped onto this
exact boulder, although they did settle
in the area.*

Chronology

4,000 – 1,000 years ago: Various African, Asian, European, and American cultures began sea travel. Early colonial empires (Egyptian, Greek, Phoenician, Roman, Chinese, Peruvian, Christian, and Islamic) developed maritime trade and warfare.

800 – 1000: Norse mariners colonized Iceland and Greenland and explored coastal North America.

1400s: Portuguese under Prince Henry began circumnavigation of Africa, seeking route to the Orient, establishing colonies, and institutionalizing slave trade.

1492: Christopher Columbus, an Italian navigator sailing for the Spanish, made his first voyage across the Atlantic.

1497: Explorer John Cabot sailed along the east coast of North America, claiming territory for England.

1524: Estevan Gomez, a Portuguese navigator sailing for the Spanish, explored the coast of New England.

1580: Englishman Francis Drake completed a circumnavigation of the globe, looting and claiming land throughout the world for England.

1586: Mathew Baker wrote *Fragments of Ancient Shipwrightery,* the first design for a sail vessel recorded on paper.

1603: Englishman Martin Pring made the first recorded European landing at Patuxet (Plymouth). Other English, French, and Dutch ships began to appear yearly in these waters. The Wampanoag were hospitable; trade was profitable and pleasing to both sides; but cultural differences, misunderstandings, and hostility became evident.

1603: King James of England began pressuring Puritans to conform to the national church. By 1607, some who refused to follow Church of England requirements began leaving for Holland.

1606: Frenchman Samuel de Champlain charted the bay at Patuxet, calling it "Port St. Louis."

1614: Captain John Smith of England named and charted New England and Plymouth. Wampanoag rights to their own homeland were not recognized.

1614: Englishman Thomas Hunt kidnapped more than 20 Wampanoag, including Tisquantum (also called Squanto), for sale as slaves.

1619: Englishman Thomas Dermer returned Tisquantum to his home.

1620: *Mayflower* voyage.

March 1621: Native leaders Samoset, Tisquantum, and Massasoit visited Plymouth and made a treaty with the English.

April 1621: *Mayflower* returned to England.

1625: Plymouth Colony began annual trading with Native people at the Kennebec River, leading to acquisition of colonial patent on lands now in the state of Maine.

1630: John Billington was the first man hanged for murder in Plymouth Colony.

1630s: Thousands of Massachusetts Bay colonists arrived, simultaneously ensuring English support and competition for Plymouth.

1684: Francis Billington died, leaving his wife with some debts and many children and grandchildren. His offspring were loyal to the colony and many became members and even leaders of the colonial church. Billington Sea, a pond in West Plymouth, still bears his family's name.

1692: Plymouth Colony became part of Massachusetts.

1700s: Shipbuilding thrived in many towns along the North River.

1820: Bicentennial celebration of *Mayflower* arrival. Pilgrim Society dedicated Pilgrim Hall Museum, relocating "Plymouth Rock" in front of it. Daniel Webster gave a famous speech praising the Pilgrims as founders of American democracy.

1863: President Lincoln declared the first national Thanksgiving Day, which has been celebrated annually ever since.

1920 – 21: Tercentennial celebration. Renovation of waterfront area around Plymouth Rock.

1947: Plimoth Plantation founded to provide an accurate representation of early Plymouth Colony.

1954: Warwick Charlton organized Project Mayflower and started fund-raising to build *Mayflower II.* Work began on July 4, 1955.

1957: *Mayflower II* sailed from Plymouth, England, to Plymouth, Massachusetts, arriving June 13. Shipmaster Alan Villiers authored two articles for *National Geographic* magazine, bringing international attention to the ship.

1970 – present: Each Thanksgiving Day, many Native people meet at the statue of Massasoit, near Plymouth Rock, to observe a National Day of Mourning.

1991 – present: After nearly three decades of inactivity, *Mayflower II* sailed six times to various ports, including Provincetown and Boston, Massachusetts, and Providence, Rhode Island.

June 2001: *Mayflower II* sailed to Boston. A National Geographic photography team went along to take pictures for this book.

2002: Billington descendants placed a historic marker on a modern office building near the site of the family's first house in the center of what has become downtown Plymouth.

Index

Illustrations are indicated by **boldface.**

Bibliography

1621: A New Look at Thanksgiving, by Catherine O'Neill Grace and Margaret M. Bruchac with Plimoth
  Plantation (National Geographic Society, 2001)
The Archaeology of Boats and Ships, An Introduction, by Basil Greenhill with John Morrison (Naval Institute
  Press, 1996)
Early Explorers of Plymouth Harbor, 1525-1619, by Henry F. Howe (Plimoth Plantation and The Pilgrim
  Society, 1953)
Memory's Nation: The Place of Plymouth Rock, by John Seelye (University of North Carolina Press, 1998)
Men, Ships, and the Sea, by Alan Villiers (National Geographic Society, 1962)
Plymouth Colony: Its History and People 1620-1691, by Eugene Aubry Stratton (Ancestry Publishing, 1986)
The Second Mayflower Adventure, by Warwick Charlton (Little, Brown & Co., 1957)
The Shipwright's Trade, by Westcott Abell (Caravan Book Service, 1962)
The Times of Their Lives: Life, Love, and Death in Plymouth Colony, by James Deetz and Patricia Scott Deetz
  (W.H. Freeman & Co., 2000)

PRIMARY SOURCE MATERIAL

Mourt's Relation: A Journal of the Pilgrims at Plymouth 1622, edited by Dwight B. Heath
  (Applewood Books, reprint 1963)
Of Plymouth Plantation 1620-1647, by William Bradford, edited by Samuel Eliot
  Morison (Alfred A. Knopf, 1952)
A Sea Grammar, by Captain John Smith (London, 1627)

Further resources available by visiting www.plimoth.org

For Sue and the girls — PA
To the memory of Warwick Charlton, and to Marietta Mullen for keeping the flame alive — JCK
For Anne Bagno, *Mayflower* descendant, companion on the journey — COG
To our children, Saskia and Calder — SB & CC

*A*CKNOWLEDGMENTS: Our thanks to the sailing crew of *Mayflower II*, especially Captain Eric Speth, John Brewster, Josh Gedraitis, Paula Marcoux, Doug Ozelius, John Reed, George Ward, and Dave Wheelock, as well as the interpretative staff of Plimoth Plantation for participation in the re-creations that allowed this story to be told. We also thank the staff of Plimoth Plantation, especially Carol City, Linda Coombs, Kathleen Curtin, Jill Hall, Marcia Hix, Liz Lodge, Marietta Mullen, Steve Pekock, Anne Phelan, Maureen Richard, Kathy Roncarati, Carolyn Travers, John Truelson, and Lisa Whalen. We are also grateful to Kendel and Mikel Carr, Charlie Mitchell and the crew of the *Jaguar*, Andy Costa and the crew of the *Andy-Lynn*, and Eric Swanson of the Cedar Hill Retreat Center.

*I*LLUSTRATIONS CREDITS: Cover, Bert Lane/Plimoth Plantation; 2-3, 8, Bert Lane/Plimoth Plantation; 12, Courtesy Thomas Gilcrease Institute of American History and Art; 45 (upper), Bert Lane/Plimoth Plantation.

Style design by Suez Kehl Corrado. The text of the book is set in Garamond. The display text is Aquiline and Chanson d'Amour.

The world's largest nonprofit scientific and educational organization, the National Geographic Society was founded in 1888 "for the increase and diffusion of geographic knowledge." Since then it has supported scientific exploration and spread information to its more than eight million members worldwide.

The National Geographic Society educates and inspires millions every day through magazines, books, television programs, videos, maps and atlases, research grants, the National Geographic Bee, teacher workshops, and innovative classroom materials.

The Society is supported through membership dues, charitable gifts, and income from the sale of its educational products.

Members receive NATIONAL GEOGRAPHIC magazine—the Society's official journal—discounts on Society products, and other benefits.

For more information about the National Geographic Society, its educational programs, and publications, or ways to support its work, please call 1-800-NGS-LINE (647-5463), or write to the following address:

National Geographic Society
1145 17th Street, N.W.
Washington, D.C. 20036-4688
U.S.A.

Visit the Society's Web site: www.nationalgeographic.com

Published by the National Geographic Society

John M. Fahey, Jr. *President and Chief Executive Officer*
Gilbert M. Grosvenor *Chairman of the Board*
Nina D. Hoffman *Executive Vice President*
President of Books and Education Publishing

Staff for this Book

Ericka Markman *Senior Vice President, President of Children's Books and Education Publishing Group*
Nancy Laties Feresten *Vice President, Editor-in-Chief, Children's Books*
Bea Jackson *Art Director, Children's Books*
Jennifer Emmett *Project Editor*
Alexandra Littlehales *Designer*
Cotton Coulson and Elizabeth LaGrua *Illustrations Editors*
Janet Dustin *Illustrations Coordinator*
Marfé Ferguson Delano *Editor*
Jo H. Tunstall *Assistant Editor*
Carl Mehler *Director of Maps*
XNR Productions *Map Research and Production*
Connie D. Binder *Indexer*
R. Gary Colbert *Production Director*
Lewis R. Bassford *Production Manager*
Vincent P. Ryan *Manufacturing Manager*

The design shown on page one and used throughout as a decorative device is a mayflower carved and painted on the stern of the *Mayflower II*.

Library of Congress Cataloging-in-Publication Data
Plimoth Plantation.
  Mayflower 1620: a new look at a pilgrim voyage / by Plimoth Plantation with Peter Arenstam, John Kemp, and Catherine O'Neill Grace; photographs by Sisse Brimberg and Cotton Coulson.
    p. cm.
  Includes index.
  ISBN: 0-7922-6142-9
  1. Mayflower (Ship)--Juvenile literature. 2. Pilgrims (New Plymouth Colony)--Juvenile literature. 3. Massachusetts--History--New Plymouth, 1620-1691--Juvenile Literature. 5. Plimoth Plantation, Inc.--Juvenile literature. [1. Mayflower (Ship) 2. Pilgrims (New Plymouth Colony) 3. Masssachusetts--History--New Plymouth, 1620-1691. 4. Mayflower II (Ship) 5. Plimoth Plantation, Inc.] I. Arenstam, Peter. II. Kemp, John. III. Grace, Catherine O'Neill, 1950- IV. Brimberg, Sisse, ill. V. Coulson, Cotton, ill. VI. Plimoth Plantation, Inc. VII. Title.
  F68.A69 2003
    974.4'8202--dc21
                                                    2002155784